MEET TONY PARKER

Basketball's Famous Point Guard

Sloan MacRae

PowerKiDS
press
New York

Published in 2009 by The Rosen Publishing Group, Inc.
29 East 21st Street, New York, NY 10010

First Edition

Editor: Amelie von Zumbusch
Book Design: Greg Tucker
Photo Researcher: Jessica Gerweck

Photo Credits: Cover, pp. 6, 11, 12, 14, 15, 16, 18, 19, 20, 22, 23, 25, 27, 28, 30 © Getty Images; pp. 5, 10 © AFP/Getty Images; pp. 8, 26 © NBAE/Getty Images.

Library of Congress Cataloging-in-Publication Data

MacRae, Sloan
    Meet Tony Parker : basketball's famous point guard / Sloan MacRae. — 1st ed.
        p. cm. — (All-star players)
    Includes index.
    ISBN 978-1-4358-2710-3 (library binding) — ISBN 978-1-4358-3102-5 (pbk.)
ISBN 978-1-4358-3108-7 (6-pack)
    1. Parker, William Anthony, 1982– —Juvenile literature. 2. Basketball players—United States—Biography—Juvenile literature. I. Title.
    GV884.P37M33 2009
    796.323092—dc22
    [B]
                                2008025281

Manufactured in the United States of America

Contents

The Point Guard from France

Tony Parker is one of the most famous **athletes** in the world. He plays point guard for the San Antonio Spurs. A point guard is a basketball team's leader on the court. A good point guard needs to be fast. Parker is one of the fastest point guards in the National Basketball Association, or NBA. At 6 feet 2 inches (1.9 m), Parker is shorter than most NBA players. Luckily, his speed makes up for his lack of height.

Parker was born in the country of Belgium, and he grew up in France. He is still a French citizen. Today, though, he has fans around the world.

All-Star Facts

Parker tried to help Paris host the 2012 Olympics. He was upset when it was announced that London would host the games instead.

Tony Parker enjoys playing for the Spurs. He has said that he likes that the members of the team work well together and share the ball.

Here, Tony Parker gets a hug from his proud father. Tony is close to his father. He has said, "My dad helps me tremendously."

Fast!

Tony Parker's mother came from the Netherlands, and his father is an American. Tony's father had played college basketball in Chicago. Then, he moved to Europe to become one of the best basketball players in France.

Even though young Tony loved to watch his father play basketball, he was more interested in soccer. Tony was not very tall, so he did not think of basketball as his sport. The great Michael Jordan changed his mind. Many people believe that Jordan was the greatest NBA player ever. Tony loved watching him play. He even got to meet Jordan on a trip to Chicago.

All-Star Facts

Tony Parker's full name is William Anthony Parker. The name "Tony" is a common nickname for Anthony.

In 2002, Parker (left) got to play against the great Michael Jordan (right) when the San Antonio Spurs played the Washington Wizards.

Tony now wanted to play basketball, but he was still not very tall. How could he play a tall person's game? Tony knew the **solution** was to be fast. He decided to **concentrate** on being a great point guard. Point guards do not have to be the tallest players on the court if they are quick enough.

Parker's hard work paid off. He was already a good point guard by the time he hit his **growth spurt** at age 15. Parker was **recruited** by the National Institute of Sport and Physical Education in Paris. Some of the biggest basketball colleges in America wanted him to play for them, too, but Parker decided to stay in France. When he was only 17, Parker became a **professional** basketball player and joined a team called Paris Basket Racing.

Before long, Parker became one of the best basketball players in the country. He was not satisfied, though. Parker wanted to play against

All-Star Facts

France's National Institute of Sport and Physical Education, or INSEP, gives the country's best young athletes a place to train and study. It is a great honor to attend INSEP.

Parker (left) is proud to be a French citizen. In 2007, he received the Legion of Honor. France's president (right) shook Parker's hand after he was given this great honor.

the best basketball players in the world. This meant coming to America to play in the NBA.

Parker entered the 2001 NBA Draft. The draft is a system that the NBA teams use to pick the best young players. Unfortunately, many of these teams had never heard of Parker. Who was this point guard from France, anyway?

In 2000, Parker took part in the Nike Hoop Summit. At this event, the best American high-school basketball players play against the best young players from around the world. Parker played very well in the game.

The San Antonio Spurs

The San Antonio Spurs decided to take a chance on Parker. This proved to be a wise decision. The Spurs were already a good team, and Parker was excited to play for them. The Spurs had won the NBA Championship only two years before. The NBA Finals is the NBA's biggest contest. It is like the Super Bowl in the NFL or the World Series in Major League Baseball.

Some young athletes would be **intimidated** to join such a great team. Parker was not. He enjoyed the challenge. Parker was just the third French person ever to play in an NBA game. Some NBA rookies need time to learn how to play against the world's top players. Parker did not need time. He led the Spurs in **assists** and steals

Parker was excited when the Spurs drafted him. He said, "It is going to be so amazing" and "playing with them is going to make the game so much easier."

Here, Parker (right) is playing in the first round of the Western Conference play-offs. The Spurs beat the Seattle SuperSonics and moved on to the semifinals.

in his rookie season. He sped up the Spurs' game and helped stars David Robinson and Tim Duncan score lots of points. Parker even became the first European selected for the NBA's All-Rookie First Team.

That season, the Spurs reached the **play-offs**. Unfortunately, they lost to the Los Angeles Lakers. Parker was not **discouraged**. He was holding his own against the best basketball players in the world. He knew he could lead the Spurs to a championship.

Throughout his time playing for the Spurs, Parker (right) has worked closely with the Spurs' head coach, Gregg Popovich (left).

Championship Ring

Parker played even better the following year. Sometimes NBA stars are **criticized** for being selfish. They hog, or refuse to pass, the ball. Parker was not selfish. He loved to find open players on the court. He made great passes to help his teammates score. Parker's **stats** were good in his rookie reason. They were even better in his second season. He helped the Spurs reach the play-offs once again.

Parker played well in the regular season, but he struggled in the **postseason**. He even spent time sitting on the bench. Postseason games are different from regular season games. Teams play harder. Players who might be **conservative** in the

Here, Parker passes the ball to a teammate during the 2003 NBA play-offs.

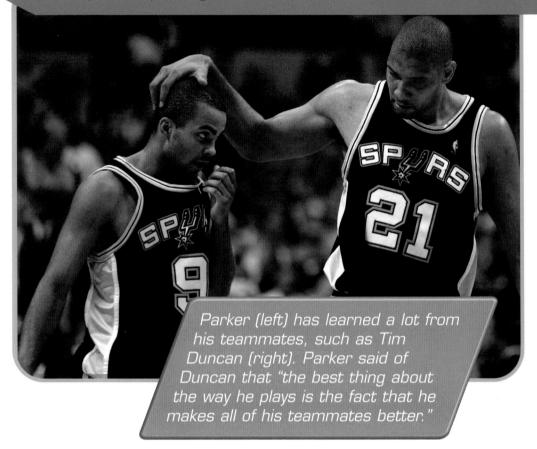

Parker (left) has learned a lot from his teammates, such as Tim Duncan (right). Parker said of Duncan that "the best thing about the way he plays is the fact that he makes all of his teammates better."

regular season hold nothing back in the play-offs. Fortunately, Parker's teammates had plenty of postseason **experience**. The Spurs beat the New Jersey Nets in the NBA Finals. Parker won his first championship ring, but he was not satisfied with his play. Spurs coach Gregg Popovich was not satisfied either. The team thought about getting a new point guard. They even tried to make a trade for the Nets' Jason Kidd. Parker told Popovich that he wanted to be the Spurs' starting point guard. Parker knew that he would have to earn that right, though.

Though it would mean lots of hard work, Parker really wanted to improve as a player and stay on as the Spurs' point guard.

Two More Rings

Parker came back and played well in his third season. The Spurs made the play-offs, but they lost once again to their **rivals**, the Lakers.

Parker and the Spurs stormed through the following season. Parker wanted to prove that he could play well in the postseason. This time, the Spurs made it through every play-off round. They faced the Detroit Pistons in the NBA Finals. The Pistons had won the championship the year before. That year, though, the entire Spurs team played well together, and Parker won his second championship ring.

In the 2005–2006 season, Parker had one of his best seasons yet. He scored more points per game than he had in any earlier season. He even

During the 2004–2005 season, Parker became an even better player. He made an average of 6.1 assists per game and scored an average of 16.6 points per game.

Parker has listened to the advice of Spurs coach Gregg Popovich and has become a much more aggressive, or forceful, player over the years.

scored more often than superstar Tim Duncan. Unfortunately, the Spurs lost in the play-offs to the Dallas Mavericks.

San Antonio reached the finals again in 2007. Parker and the Spurs faced LeBron James and the Cleveland Cavaliers. Some experts believed that James was the best player in basketball. However, Parker and the Spurs **swept** James and the Cavaliers. Parker was named the finals Most Valuable Player, or MVP. This meant he had done more for his team than any other player. He was the first European ever to be named MVP.

Parker proudly lifted his MVP trophy, or award, over his head on June 14, 2007. The happy player said of his win, "It's great, it's great. It's just unbelievable. I'm speechless."

Basketball is not all that Parker cares about. Family is very important to him. While Parker looked up to Michael Jordan when he was young, his father has always been his hero. To this day, Tony and his father speak on the phone after every single Spurs game. Tony's father helps him improve. Tony is also close to his younger brothers, T. J. and Pierre. Both brothers are also great basketball players. Tony hopes they will follow in his footsteps and join the NBA.

His parents are now divorced, but Tony also keeps in touch with his mother. She used to be a model but is now a health food coach. She helps

All-Star Facts

Even though his mother tells him to eat well, Tony Parker hates spinach and cauliflower. He is a big fan of French food.

Because his wife, Eva Longoria Parker, is a famous actress, Tony Parker gets to go to lots of award shows and movie premieres, or openings.

Parker also works with programs that encourage kids to read. In 2003, he gave several young fans copies of The Little Prince. The Little Prince, *which was written by a French author,* was one of Parker's favorite books as a child.

people stay healthy by eating food that is good for them. Tony knows it is important for star athletes to stay healthy by eating well.

In 2007, Tony Parker got married. His wife is as famous as he is. She is an American actress named Eva Longoria Parker. Their wedding reception, or party, took place in a castle outside of Paris.

Tony Parker also likes to help people. He gives 20 tickets to each Spurs home game to children from poor families. Parker works for the French branch of the Make-A-Wish-Foundation, too. Make-A-Wish is a worldwide charity that helps children who are sick.

Here, Parker and his mother are attending a 2007 event to raise money for the Make-A-Wish Foundation.

Three Rings and Counting

Thanks to Parker, the Spurs are on their way to becoming a **dynasty**. A sports team is called a dynasty when it wins several championships in a very short time. Most NBA players never win a championship ring. It did not take Parker long to win three. He came close to winning his fourth in 2008. Unfortunately, though, the Spurs lost in the play-offs to the Lakers.

Most people think 6 feet 2 inches (1.9 m) is tall. It is not tall for a basketball superstar. However, Parker has proved that being fast can make up for not being very tall. He is one of the best and fastest point guards in NBA history.

Tony Parker has always been quick, but he has worked hard to become a great team player, too. He has also become more aggressive and more consistent.

Height: 6' 2" (1.9 m)
Weight: 180 pounds (82 kg)
Team: San Antonio Spurs
Position: Point guard
Uniform Number: 9
Date of Birth: May 17, 1982

2007–2008 Season Stats

Games Played	3-Point Percentage	Free-Throw Percentage	Rebounds per Game	Assists per Game	Points per Game
69	.258	.715	3.2	6	18.8

NBA Career Stats as of Summer 2008

Games Played	3-Point Percentage	Free-Throw Percentage	Rebounds per Game	Assists per Game	Points per Game
540	.314	.716	3.1	5.5	16

Glossary

assists (uh-SISTS) Passes that help a teammate score points.

athletes (ATH-leets) People who take part in sports.

concentrate (KON-sen-trayt) To focus one's thoughts and attention on one thing.

conservative (kun-SER-vuh-tiv) Not wanting to take risks.

criticized (KRIH-tuh-syzd) Found fault with.

discouraged (dis-KUR–ijd) Feeling unsure or uncertain.

dynasty (DY-nas-tee) A powerful group that keeps its position for a long time.

experience (ik-SPEER-ee-ents) Knowledge or skill gained by doing or seeing something.

growth spurt (GROHTH SPURT) A time when a person or thing grows quickly.

intimidated (in-TIH-muh-dayt-ed) Made shy or afraid.

play-offs (PLAY-ofs) Games played after the regular season ends to see who will play in the championship game.

postseason (pohst-SEE-zun) Games played after the regular season.

professional (pruh-FESH-nul) Having to do with someone who is paid for what he or she does.

recruited (rih-KROOT-ed) Chosen to join a group.

rivals (RY-vulz) Two people or teams who try to get or to do the same thing as one another.

solution (suh-LOO-shun) An answer to a problem.

stats (STATS) Facts about players in the form of numbers.

swept (SWEPT) Won all stages of a game or contest.

Index

Web Sites

Due to the changing nature of Internet links, PowerKids Press has developed an online list of Web sites related to the subject of this book. This site is updated regularly. Please use this link to access the list:

www.powerkidslinks.com/asp/tonyp/